JOURNEY TO THE PAST

MAYAN TIKAL

Romano Solbiati

RAINTREE
STECK-VAUGHN
PUBLISHERS

A Harcourt Company

Austin · New York
www.steck-vaughn.com

Published by Raintree Steck-Vaughn, an imprint of Steck-Vaughn Company

Library of Congress Cataloging-in-Publication Data

Solbiati, Romano
    Mayan Tikal / Romano Solbiati.
        p. cm. — (Journey to the past)
    Includes bibliographical references and index.
    ISBN 0-7398-1955-0
        1. Tikal Site (Guatemala)—Juvenile literature. 2. Mayas—Juvenile literature.
[1. Mayas. 2. Indians of Central Amercia—Guatemala.]   I. Title.   II. Series.

F1435.1.T5 S65 2001
972.81'2—dc21   00-045924

Editorial Coordinator: Cristina Drago
Editor: Stefano Sibella
Translated by: David Stein

Illustrations: Aldo Ripamonti
Graphics: Marco Volpati
Cover: Max Brinkmann

Raintree Steck-Vaughn Staff: Shirley Shalit, Pam Wells
Project Manager: Lyda Guz
Photo Research: Claudette Landry, Sarah Fraser

Photo Credits:

P.48a ©Gail SHumway/FPG International; p.48b ©Kuhn, Lee/FPG International; pp.49a, 49b ©Robert Fried; p.50a ©Suzanne Murphy-Larronde/FPG International; p.50b ©Haroldo Castro/FPG International; p.51a ©Robert Fried; p.51b ©Pcholkin, Vladimir/FPG International.

All other photographs are from the Archives of IGDA.

Printed in Italy

1 2 3 4 5 6 7 8 9 04 03 02 01

TABLE OF CONTENTS

Few Roads Lead to Tikal!

Mayab, the country of the Mayans, has the shape of a large triangle stretched between two oceans, the Atlantic and the Pacific, and measures more than 115,830 square miles in area. To the south, it is closed off by an almost impassable barrier of mountains and volcanoes. The rest of the country consists of a series of lowlands threaded by winding rivers and covered by thick, dense forests. The climate is tropical—very hot and damp—with seemingly endless rain. The only exceptions to this climate are in the north and in the Motagua hollow where the air is a little dryer.

Mayab

N

Gulf of Mexico

Uucyabnal
(Chichén Itza)

Uxmal

(Yucatán)

Palenque •

Usumacinta

• Tikal

Yaxchilán

Quiriguá • *Motagua*

Kaminaljuyú

Copán

Pacific Ocean

Tikal, the largest Mayan city of the Classical Period, is located just about in the middle of the lowland region. Although almost all the main connecting roads, both within the Mayab and leading to it, meet here, getting to Tikal will not be easy for you. First, because of the thick forest with its trees that reach heights of 160 feet, you can easily get lost. Second, there are very few helpful paths.

The Mayans have no beasts of burden, and have never discovered the wheel. So their only means of transportation is going on foot. You can arrange to be carried on someone's shoulders. Or you may prefer to ride in a portable chair that is carried on poles by two men. But besides being tiring, these methods will take endless amounts of time.

There is a paved highway system (the *sacbeob*), which, however, does not cover great distances. The most efficient means of travel is the canoe. Canoes can travel along the shore or the rivers, and through the extensive network of canals created by the Mayans.

However, the main obstacle in your journey is the Mayan culture itself. The Mayans have an intense distrust of outsiders. Also, the various cities of the region are in a constant state of conflict. Travelers face very high risks from warring groups. The best way to arrive safe and sound at your destination and avoid human as well as nature's dangers is to join a local group of traders. They will be traveling with special safe-conduct passes and armed guards. Good luck!

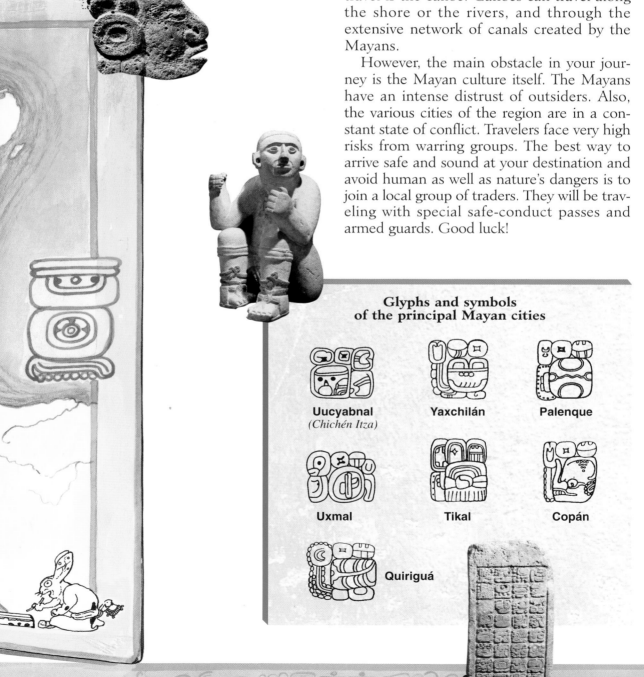

Glyphs and symbols of the principal Mayan cities

Uucyabnal
(*Chichén Itza*)

Yaxchilán

Palenque

Uxmal

Tikal

Copán

Quiriguá

Welcome!

You will recognize it immediately! The skyline of Tikal is unlike any other! Even at a great distance, you cannot miss the reddish color of the pyramids. They are several stories high and cover whole city blocks. These large structures have steep, sloping walls with openings, covered walkways, and terraces that meet and cross one another in a complicated and varied design. You will see large squares containing beautiful gardens. You will see more pyramids, other palaces, and public buildings where markets are held, groups gather, and ball games are played. You will be amazed at the canals, cisterns, and reservoirs of water. But you will be especially impressed by the famous paved Mayan streets, white as snow, blinding in the sunlight, extending for a width of 26 feet.

However, what you have seen so far is only one part of the city, the one that we shall call the historic center, the formal, ceremonial center of Tikal. The parts of the city where most of the people live are scattered, or hidden in the forest.

Some of the Mayans fear that the forest itself is suffering from overuse. They have come to depend on it so completely.

A diffuse city

How big is Tikal? The historic center, with its pyramids and palaces, is large but not enormous. It covers about 8 square miles. But the entire city is vast, almost ten times as large as the center. In all directions there are clearings where you will see groups of houses, villages, and small towns with their own little ceremonial centers. The fact is that the Mayans collect in large family groups, or clans that lead shared lives. The members are all related and make up separate, small worlds connected to the rest of the community by their language, their markets, and their religious ceremonies.

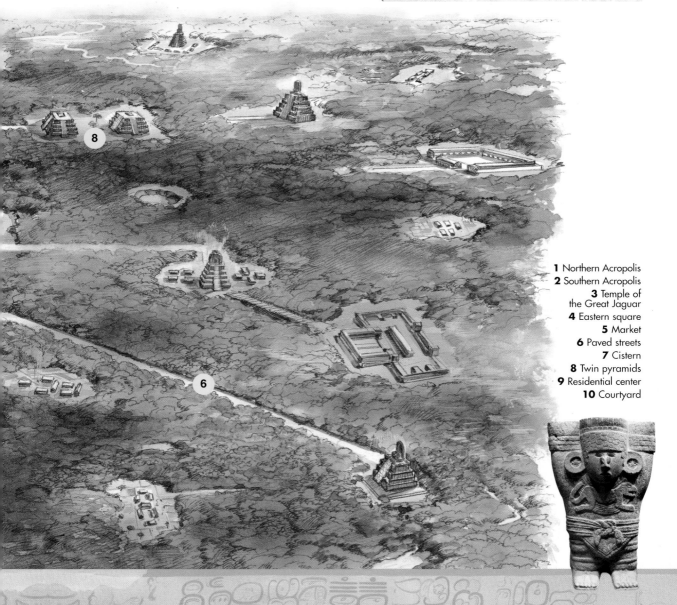

1 Northern Acropolis
2 Southern Acropolis
3 Temple of the Great Jaguar
4 Eastern square
5 Market
6 Paved streets
7 Cistern
8 Twin pyramids
9 Residential center
10 Courtyard

Useful Information

In Mayab, the Mayan region, the first thing that you must acquire is a safe-conduct pass. Do not take this matter lightly. The Mayans usually are polite with outsiders but they are also very distrustful and suspicious toward anyone who crosses their borders. Going around their territory without a permit kept well in view can cause unpleasant, if not fatal, consequences. Since you have probably reached Tikal together with a group of merchants—there is no other means of reasonably safe travel in Mayan territory—ask how to obtain this "permit." But don't think that it is a matter of a piece of paper with writing and a stamp or a seal. Around these parts writing is only used for political or religious purposes. Here a permit or safe-conduct pass is essentially an ornament. It could be a pendant, a breast pin, or an armband on which the symbol of the person who granted permission has been engraved. It is something of a good luck or protective object.

The other important thing that you should know is that in Tikal as in any other Mayan city, it is necessary to heed the rules of behavior, often difficult to follow even on the part of the natives themselves. For example, one may not go out after sunset without special permission and only with an escort. Also, certain areas cannot be visited during particular seasons of the year or during certain anniversaries. It may not be permitted to visit temples, sanctuaries, or courts unless accompanied by a priest or other high official. It is a very good idea to find someone from the area who can serve as a guide.

MONEY

The products most often used by the Mayans as a means of exchange or money are cocoa, jade, and some varieties of seashells considered to be particularly rare and precious. The most widespread and generally accepted currency is without a doubt cocoa. Its seeds, beside possessing a high economic value, are light, manageable, and easy to transport. If you want to shop, you should get a special kind of leather purse that will hold 8,000 grains of cocoa. You can wear it on your shoulder or around your waist. Jade beads are highly prized, but their value varies greatly according to the quality of the stone, and you have to be an expert to know this. On some occasions, you can use gold necklaces from Central America. Mayans are not very fond of gold, however. They call it "the sun's waste material."

WHERE TO EAT AND SLEEP?

Get used to it. In the Mayab there is nothing that looks at all like an inn or a restaurant. In the center of town you can, however, find lodging in the foreign quarter, which is used for the most part by merchants and traveling craftsmen. To sleep here, you do not have to pay anything (it is considered a public service) but you will have to get your own food and even prepare your own meals. The situation is better in the small, rural communities that make up the city's outlying areas. Here hospitality is sacred and you will be treated like a member of the family with your meals included. Consider yourself fortunate if a high official or member of the court asks you out. You may get a chance to see certain festivals and enjoy the great banquets that usually accompany them. But there are also days of total fasting. Give them your full respect.

ADDRESSES

In Tikal, as in any other Mayan city, you will not find street names or numbers. If you are looking for an address, you must rely on your common sense and your sense of direction. In the center you find plenty of landmarks. For example, there are the acropolises. There are the three huge groups of many buildings, temples, and palaces for the upper class. There are also the squares, the marketplace, and the twin pyramids.

Things get complicated if you have to get to one of the outer locations, since a large portion of the city is almost hidden in the forest. It is of little use to create a map of the area or to wait to get information from a passerby. Aside from the fact that the points of the compass are arranged differently with respect to ours (east is up, west is down, south to the right, and north to the left), no pedestrian would ever talk to a stranger. The frequent rains often alter the landscape, changing the shape of the terrain. It would be best for you to use a guide.

CLOTHING

Mayan clothing is both basic and refined. The main male garment is the *ex,* or loincloth. It is made of rough material for the lower classes and of fine cotton decorated with bright needlework for the ruling classes. Its length and the richness of its design vary according to the social class. A cloak, which is tied at the shoulder, serves as a blanket for the poor. The typical feminine dress is the *manta,* a tunic sewn along the sides with openings for the head and arms. It is sometimes worn with a petticoat or a shawl *(boach),* of varying degrees of richness according to social class. Almost everyone wears sandals made of animal skin or cord. Most Mayans wear various ornaments, such as nose and lip rings, earrings, bracelets, and ankle bands made of precious materials. The feather headdresses made from the rare *quetzal* or from the macaw, like leopard or deer cloaks, are worn only by the ruler or the aristocracy.

Take note: Everyone, absolutely everyone, exhibits at least one tattoo. It usually denotes the clan to which one belongs, but it also has religious and magical meanings. If the family who "adopts" you as a guest offers to give you a tattoo, do not refuse. They could be offended!

HOW TO CURE YOURSELF IF YOU GET SICK?

If by chance you should happen to feel sick and have to seek medical help, get ready. If you are lucky, you will find at your bedside a pair of strange-looking characters, one with a stern and serious appearance carrying a book under his arm. The other is holding a bell made of rattlesnake skin and some small bags of very strange objects. The first of these men is sort of a cross between a prophet and an astrologer. In his book he will look up things that have to do with the date of your birth, and throwing some pebbles on the ground, he will make up a kind of horoscope-prophecy, revealing the dark forces at the root of your sickness. At this point the other character will go into action. This is the shaman, or medicine-man, who will have already decided what is wrong with you, using a kind of crystal ball. He will begin to sprinkle you with water, shaking his bell and dancing around you while singing a slow, mournful song. Then he will touch your body at precise points, throwing on the ground a great variety of unusual objects, such as bones and animal parts, bird feathers and beaks. Finally, he will give you some herbs as medicine. Or he will drain some of your blood by applying a few leeches, or blood-sucking worms, to your body. Although all this will seem strange to you, you will begin to feel better. Actually, the Mayan "doctors" are not frauds or amateurs. They have been practicing their arts for thousands of years.

WHAT TO EAT IN TIKAL?

The basic element of the Mayan diet is corn. You find it used in all preparations: in the form of tortillas, round flat bread made of cornmeal flour filled with meat and/or vegetables; or in the form of tamales, ground meat wrapped in cornmeal dough and steamed. Corn is also used in refreshing beverages, or in alcoholic ones (*balche*). When they can, the citizens combine with the corn two other local products—beans and the powerful red pepper (*chili*). Chili is also used as a medicine because of its numbing or pain-relieving effect. The cooking of the wealthy classes employs a large variety of foods, from game to the flesh of some semidomestic animals, such as deer, pheasants, turkeys, tapirs, peccaries, and agoutis.

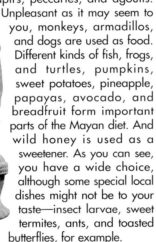

Unpleasant as it may seem to you, monkeys, armadillos, and dogs are used as food. Different kinds of fish, frogs, and turtles, pumpkins, sweet potatoes, pineapple, papayas, avocado, and breadfruit form important parts of the Mayan diet. And wild honey is used as a sweetener. As you can see, you have a wide choice, although some special local dishes might not be to your taste—insect larvae, sweet termites, ants, and toasted butterflies, for example.

There are two Mayan products you will probably not complain about. The Mayab is the country of cocoa, from which chocolate is made, and of *chicle*, from which chewing gum is made. A bit of advice, however, concerning cocoa: Here it is mixed with cold water and flavored with a large amount of hot pepper. A real bomb!

WHERE TO GO SHOPPING?

Do not look for stores or shops in Tikal or anywhere else in the Mayab. You will not find any. In all the Mayan city-states commerce is centralized, which amounts to saying that it is controlled directly by the local powers. The only retail business permitted is the one that takes place at certain times in the people's markets, under the supervision of public officials. This guarantees the quality and the fair price of many products. But the system severely limits the number and social class of those who can buy the goods, especially the most valued ones. If you are not interested in absolutely necessary products or manufactured goods of little value, such as baskets, vases, rough woven cloth, necklaces made of bone or wood, and tools, you must employ the services of an agent, or go-between. He will have to be a member of the aristocracy. In fact, the production and sales of luxury products such as jade, decorated and painted ceramics, and other rare and costly goods, are a monopoly of the aristocratic class exclusively. One thing that you may neither buy nor take with you—the feathers of the quetzal. They are sacred and possession of them by an outsider is a sacrilege punishable by death.

NUMBER SYSTEM

The Mayan numbers are at first glance very simple. The ones are written with dots, fives with a line, and zeros with a kind of flower or seashell. For example, to write 4, you put four dots in a row, to write 6, you make a line with a dot above it, for 10 two lines one on top of the other and so on until you reach 19. With 20, things change. You either write a zero with a dot above it or use a special sign. Why? Because the Mayan's system is not based on tens, but rather on twenties. This can complicate your calculations enormously when you make purchases. If you count by 10s the multiples of 10 are 100, 1,000, 10,000, and so on. Counting by 20 as the Mayans do, the multiples of 20 become 400, 8,000, 160,000, and so forth. It makes your head spin! So get help from someone while shopping and in any case, be trusting. The Mayans are honest people.

TIME AND THE CALENDAR

For the Mayans, time measurement has to do with magical and religious needs, rather than practical ones. For them, time is a living entity which influences both the rhythms of the universe and the fate of every single person. The hours of the day (*kin*) are divided into 13 daytime and 9 nighttime hours. They are distributed this way on the basis of the "heavenly spheres" or the "subterranean kingdom" that is governing the world at a given moment.

Things get even more complicated when it comes to the calendars. The Mayans have two—the *haab* or ordinary, solar almanac of 365 days and the *tzolkin* or sacred year of 260 days. The basis of the tzolkin is a series of special religious days. The haab on the other hand consists of a time period (*tun*) of 18 "god-months," each one lasting 20 days, in addition to a period of 5 days, considered to be an unlucky time. In order to compute periods of time greater than one year, the Mayans use several methods. One of them is based on the 18-month year whose larger unit, the *katun* (20 tun) is considered very important.

BABIES IN TIKAL

You will notice that all Mayans have a flat and unusually long head as well as a slight squint. These are not natural, but are purposely produced features. Soon after birth the baby's head is bandaged and placed between two strips of wood for several days so that the skull is gently pressed. The Mayans do this so that the infant's head will look as much as possible like the head of the corn god, which has the shape of a corncob. The squint is achieved by hanging a marble in front of the eyes of the baby to produce a somewhat cross-eyed effect. The Mayans feel that this look is a mark of beauty.

Although they are adored (mothers nurse their babies until the age of four), Mayan babies are treated a little roughly. While they are young, they must have their ears, nose, and lips pierced to hold the ornaments that they will put on as adults. For the slightest mistake, they are punished severely—pinches and pepper in the eyes for the girls; beatings with stinging or prickly plants for the boys. Of special interest is the fact that shortly after they stop nursing, the children go to work to help the adults.

THE MAYANS, WHAT CHARACTERS!

At first, Mayans seem to look like teenagers. They are thin and short—five feet is average for men, eight inches less for the average woman. They seem to be rather quiet and slow, so you could easily make the mistake of thinking them shy. Actually, they are mature adults strengthened physically by a harsh and difficult life, whose seemingly shy nature is nothing other than a natural caution mixed with pride.

It is not easy to gain a Mayan's trust. It is even more difficult to try to enter the Mayan world. Do you want an example? Try to ask a Mayan his name. He will reveal his date of birth, which corresponds to his first name when he was a baby. He will even tell you his last name and his mother's maiden name, as well as the nickname given to him when he was a boy. But his real name, acquired in his passage to adulthood, he will never tell to you because it would be like betting his last dollar, risking everything he had.

In addition Mayan society, where political, religious, military, and economic power go hand in hand, is closed and rigid like few others. Every city of some importance, like Tikal, forms a regional kingdom that constitutes a universe unto itself. It has its own sovereign (*ahau*) who is often the high priest. Under him are the nobles, warriors, and merchants, that is to say, the aristocracy or local elite whose members are usually related to each other. The mass of citizens form the common people. This also forms the lowest rung of society because the slaves do not have a social ranking.

The Northern Acropolis

You have to enter Tikal almost on tiptoe, with reverence, with all the respect due one of the most sacred places in the universe. It would be best to arrive at a moment of grace—at sunset, under a leaden sky streaked by lightening, the air sultry and heavy, shaking from the roar of the thunder. You would then feel the huge platform of the Northern Acropolis vibrating and you would see it swaying like an island suspended between heaven and earth. In the blood-red pyramids, whipped by the rain, and in the disorderly rows of steles—stone monuments to the memory of revered kings—you might understand the profound soul of Tikal.

Here is a world of the dead in the heart of a city of the living. In the pyramids and the steles of the Northern Acropolis, the memory of generations is preserved, their spirit, their traditions, their constantly renewed ties with the world of the gods and with the eternal laws of the universe. Here, an ancient world lives on, its strength constantly renewed, thanks to the memory and devotions of the Mayans, and, according to Mayan belief, thanks to the sacrifice of the human hearts that lie buried in the base of the pyramids and the steles.

LIGHTENING, ANTS, AND CORN

Listen to this ancient Mayan story.
Way back in time, all the world's corn in the world was piled under a mountain of rock. One day, while digging an underground passageway, the ants discovered the hiding place and began to carry the corn away. The wolf found out about it and told the other animals as well as humans. Nobody, however, except for the ants, managed to get to the corn. So, the humans begged the gods of rain for help. The rain-gods hurled a lightening bolt against the mountain. The mountain opened and everybody was able to carry away the corn. But the heat of the lightening bolt had toasted the plants. That is why there are four kinds of corn: black, red, yellow and white.

The Shadow Line

You may already understand the idea that the border between life and death in the Mayab is dim and barely sensed like the shadow line, the line between night and day, at twilight. It is not by chance that the dead are often buried under the floor of their own house.

The Central Acropolis

What is so surprising about the Central Acropolis is the fact that it rises up and dominates the capital of the kingdom like an immense, inaccessible fortress. Its outer surfaces display multicolored decorations which appear to make up grooves that form delicate designs. However you will be most impressed by the grandeur of the entire structure.

You will realize that you are facing a city within a city, or better, the heart of the city. In fact, the Central Acropolis is the political, religious, cultural, and administrative center of Tikal. Here, concentrated in a maze of levels, courtyards, terraces, gardens, corridors, and buildings, are all the most important residences of the elite Mayan ruling class. Here are the lodgings of the royal family, the homes of the high nobility, the chapel-monas-teries of the priests, and the houses of men and those of the women (see page 20, 22). Here also is where the aristocratic heirs live together. In the same area are the large collective warehouses that guard the resources of the community.

The Central Acropolis is really a city-palace that in some way reflects the Mayan idea of the world in which everything is hinged onto a central axis, a fixed line. On the highest floor of the Central Acropolis—the axis—is the throne room. It is here that the ahau receives foreign ambassadors, dispenses justice, acts as the high priest, and decides between war and peace. Almost a king-god combination.

The Symbols of Power

If you have the good fortune to be received at court, admire the richness of the king's robes and those of his principal wife. They are made of fine fabrics and decorated with a wealth of jade and the feathers of the macaw and of the precious quetzal. In the midst of this grand display take special notice of the royal scepter. It is an emblem of Bolon Tzacab, "Nine Generations." He is the god, half man, half snake, who protects the generations of the ruling families through the ages. Notice also the curious multi-pointed knife worn by the sovereign. It is a symbol of the jaguar's claws. Some said that the king always wears a mysterious leather case around his neck. The case holds a sacred stone inherited from his ancestors. That stone proves his hereditary power and his right to rule.

A HIGHLY REGARDED GUEST

What would a dwarf be doing at court? Is he perhaps the jester? Not at all. Dwarfs are held in high regard by the Mayans and treated with great respect and reverence. They believe that the deformed body of a dwarf bears a resemblance to a god. That is why dwarfs are always respected guests.

The Temple of the Jaguar

The tallest pyramid in all of the Mayab is 196 feet high and towers over the ceremonial center. It is a symbol of the great city of Tikal. Rising from its top is a famous temple. While the building does not have a precise name, it is mostly called the "Temple of the Great Jaguar." The people of Tikal believe that the temple is an open door to the beyond, to the world of gods and spirits. Ordinary people and even low-ranking priests are not allowed to enter this holy place. The kings and high priests meet there only for solemn ceremonies which, except for those that end in large sacrifices, take place in the inside halls of the temple out of public view. Usually less important sacred ceremonies are held elsewhere—in the household sanctuaries near the minor temples and especially in the chapel-monastery of the Central Acropolis.

In the Temple of the Great Jaguar, student-priests subject themselves to painful trials to harden their body and to strengthen their spirit. The physical hardships are an exercise that prepares the priests to enter into contact with the invisible powers that govern the universe. Such encounters normally occur in the magical atmosphere of night vigils.

The Jaguar Sun

For the Mayans the jaguar, besides being a noble animal, is a symbol of strength and power, and consequently, of royalty. The jaguar also represents the sun in its nighttime journey through the sky. It is then that it ventures into the obscure regions of the afterlife, in order to be reborn at dawn in the world of humans. That is why, Mayans looking at a starstudded sky perceive the outline of a jaguar. Its spotted coat is formed by the sometimes strong and intense, sometimes weak and barely twinkling stars.

The Eastern Square and the Market

If you want to make good purchases in Tikal, the ideal place is the great square located some hundred meters east of the Central Acropolis. Here stands a vast group of buildings, an authentic commercial village, with both stores and stands. Here, during the great feasts, foreign and local merchants along with artists, craftsmen, scribes, medicine men, and others meet to show their wares and to offer their services. Naturally the Mayans who connect the market to shops are all members of the upper class, since the working classes, especially those of the farm villages, rarely use the markets. The Tikal marketplace is open especially to men, although it is not uncommon to see women, most of whom work for aristocratic families, doing their shopping here.

The merchandise may come from very far away. The highest priced goods are the artworks done with feathers or stone. Among the most valuable items are knife blades of volcanic glass, necklaces in jade and other hard stones, and ceramic vases. It is normal to see between the ware-covered mats, healers ready to make quick diagnoses and to offer miraculous remedies. The money being used to pay for these goods or services? The usual: cocoa seeds, jade beads, and seashells.

Work as money

At the market, if you do not have anything to pay with? It's no problem. You can always offer—in exchange for what interests you—your muscles. Your offer will be hard to refuse. The Mayans have a strong sense of community and are used to exchanging offers of work for goods.

THE FEAST OF HONEY

If you arrive in Tikal in the fifth month of the Mayan solar calendar, you will see the Eastern Square become a golden, fantastic, and constantly changing scene. The entire month is dedicated to the god of the bees. In order to gain his favor, the beekeepers of the region search their supplies to offer him delicious portions of all their different products. For the priests and persons of a certain age, they offer the powerful liquor, balche. Not to be missed at any cost!

The Men's House

Do you want to attend a wrestling match, see how a jaguar is tamed, or participate in a forest hunt? Ask permission to visit the men's house. What is this place? It's kind of a halfway measure between a school and a college where the young aristocratic males go to live once they've entered their teenage years. They stay there until they are ready to marry, about their twentieth year. The purpose of the House is to educate the future members of the Mayan governing class and prepare them for the roles and duties that they will be called on to perform as adults.

The atmosphere is pleasant but plain, the discipline severe, and the treatment the same for everyone. But careful attention is paid to promoting individual strengths. Thus, the young men who show outstanding religious interests are quickly sent to the monastery-chapel, while those who show artistic or commercial talent are entrusted to teachers of writing and mathematics. All of them undergo severe physical and moral training ranging from frequent fasts and ritual sacrifices to martial arts and survival exercises.

Everything is aimed at cultivating what are considered the greatest virtues of a Mayan noble—a sense of personal limitations, respect for others, disdain for pain, and personal dignity. A bore? Perhaps. But you try to survive an entire week by yourself in the forest with no other tool within your reach but your hands, as these thirteen- and fourteen-year-olds do.

THE HUNT OF THE QUETZAL

The quetzal is a rare, stupendous bird whose tail feathers are an ornament sought by kings and high dignitaries. Its capture, using a blowpipe, represents a great undertaking for a noble youth. Once the precious feathers have been removed, the bird must be set free because he is a sacred animal. Killing a quetzal is punishable by death.

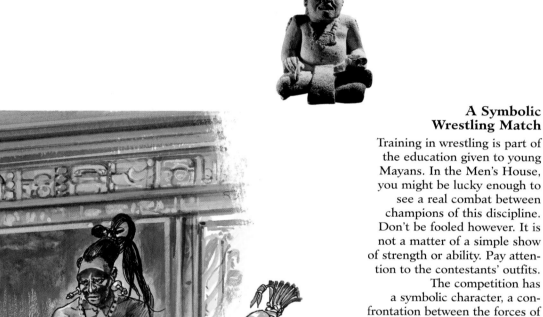

A Symbolic Wrestling Match

Training in wrestling is part of the education given to young Mayans. In the Men's House, you might be lucky enough to see a real combat between champions of this discipline. Don't be fooled however. It is not a matter of a simple show of strength or ability. Pay attention to the contestants' outfits.

The competition has a symbolic character, a confrontation between the forces of heaven, symbolized by an outfit that includes bird feathers, and the forces of the lower world, represented by the coat of the jaguar, the "nighttime sun."

The Women's House

The young female members of the Mayan aristocracy are also forced to quickly leave their family to enter the Women's House. They stay there until they are old enough to marry. The rules that they must obey are more or less the same ones found in the Men's House—community living, severe discipline, and equal treatment for all. The final goal is also the same—to form the future ruling class.

Some Mayan sovereigns and high priests are women. However, the content of the education given in this place is different. Although none of the young noblewomen living in the Women's House will ever have to work, they must still learn to do the same tasks that concern a simple peasant—tidying up rooms, washing clothing, grinding corn on the metate, and cooking. These are boring chores that involve early rising and unpleasant drudgery.

In addition, since they are aristocrats, they have extra chores tied to their social class—getting up at night to burn copale to the gods, learning to shape ceramics, spin

cotton, weave mantas, and decorate and beautify the rooms of the House. Such tasks exercise the spirit of sacrifice and dedication typical of the Mayan women. It is a good rule among the upper Mayan classes to learn to perform all the daily taks and to obey before learning to command and to direct.

Itzamná

You will often see iguanas in the arms of Mayan women for whom these animals are not reptiles. Rather they are the symbol of Itzamná, the father of all the gods, the creator of the human race, and protector of the nobility, whose name literally means "house of the iguana."

Ixchel and the dream

The Women's House is under the protection of Ixchel, the goddess of the rainbow. In addition, she is goddess of the moon, magic, and fertility. She is also the wife of Itzamná. It is indeed said that the multicolored designs with which the Mayan women decorate their manta are all her work. How is this possible? Simple: Ixchell appears in the dreams of the women who most venerate her, showing them from time to time which theme they must weave into the cloth. Consequently, when you buy a Mayan fabric, remember that you are not acquiring a mere piece of cloth, but a divine dream.

The rural dwellings

I don't know if you have noticed, but in the countryside around Tikal you don't find a house—a single house by itself. Wherever you go, you find small rural settlements of not less than three or four dwellings or real villages populated by tens or hundreds of persons. The reason is clear: To survive for very long alone in the midst of a tropical forest is practically impossible. That is why the Mayan peasants encourage and support a strong community spirit and a great attachment to the family. These two characteristics tend to go together since the Mayan family unit is of the extended type—a large clan that includes not only different generations but many relatives acquired through marriage or adoption.

The risk that you take visiting a peasant community is finding yourself facing a wall of distrust, if not hostility. However there is a benefit in that once the initial first strangeness is overcome, you are adopted like a son, and surrounded with endless

attentions. From that moment on, you are protected by the entire group at all times. Remember, however: once you have become part of a Mayan family, don't think that you can stand around loafing. Here everyone is used to working, to helping each other, whether it be a case of taking care of the crops, hunting, fishing, or attending to small domestic chores. This also holds true for the guests of the house, naturally. Have courage.

"YOUR GRACE," CORN

Do not be amazed if you see a peasant woman kneel down and talk respectfully to an ear of corn, going so far as to offer it *copale.* The fact is that corn is considered a great god—Yum Kaas, the most beautiful of the Mayan gods, the one who gave rise to the human body.

Milpa

The natural resources that surround Tikal are decidedly generous. In the forest you can pick delicious tropical fruits that grow wild like papaya or avocado. You can hunt deer and wild turkey. You must, however, always guard against the traps that the forest hides—snakes, mosquitoes, ants, and insects that make their way under your skin. However, the forest's resources are not enough to feed a large population. To remedy this, the Mayan peasants periodically clear and burn some portions of the forest, creating soil fertilized by the ashes, where they can cultivate corn, beans, and whatever they wish. These fields taken from the forest are called *milpa.*

The Game of Palla

They call it *pok-ta-pok*. It is considered the national game of the Mayans although other people played it before them and its origins go way back in time. The word pok-ta-pok captures perfectly the dry and hard sound of the rubber ball, a little bigger than a basketball, which violently pounds everything that it strikes, players included. That is why the athletes who step onto the field are armed as if they were headed for battle, with helmets, shin guards, leather armbands, and strong chest and abdomen protectors.

The rules are simple. Two teams of three or more players must succeed in carrying the palla into the adversary's field with the aim of sending it through a stone ring overhead.

The spectacle is exciting and seems to be almost an acrobatic game, since the players can strike the palla with their elbows, arms, hips, and knees, but not their hands or feet. But is it really a game? They say that it is not, that in reality it is a religious ritual that symbolizes the eternal conflict between the forces of good and evil. It also seems that the captain or one of the players of the defeated team is sacrificed at the end of the game, although not in public. The players of pok-ta-pok are not your everyday guys, but rather nobles or figures of high social

standing in Tikal or in a competing city, which might give the game a political significance. You figure it out. In any case, enjoy the contest. It is really unique.

THE XIBALBÁ AND THE DIVINE TWINS

According to an ancient legend, the game of palla might have had its origin in a challenge between the gods of the Mayan afterlife and the Divine Twins, Hunapú and Ixbalanqué. The defeat and the sacrifice of the twins at the end of the game might have coincided with the birth of the human race.

The "Palla-Sun"

For many Mayans, the game of palla has a magical significance and could serve to predict the future. The movements of the palla, in fact, resemble those of the sun, seen from time to time as a kindly macaw, daytime star-divinity, or as an unlucky jaguar. It all depends on the area of the field where the palla falls. From the movement of the game, the Mayan priests are then in a position to predict if the coming days or months of the year will be of good or bad fortune.

The Muluc
New Year

Not all Mayan New Years are the same. Every new year begins on a day named after a god who is the bearer of fortune, who can be either good or bad. Completely unfavorable are the years that begin with the god-days Ix and Cahuac, bearers respectively of drought and of storms. Omens are favorable if the years begin with Kan, one of the aspects of the god of corn or with Muluc, god-day of the moon which brings rain and fertility. The celebrations that inaugurate the Muluc years are particularly lively and joyous since they are linked to the expectation of good harvests. Usually they begin with the sacrifice of a turkey dedicated to the father of the gods, Itzamná.

The happy nature of the event involves group activities of a popular kind, although no woman may take part. As on other occasions, you can see the student priests, painted in the colors of the cardinal points from Mayan mythology. (East is red; north, white; west, black; and south, yellow.) The

priests confront each other in the fire dance, walking barefoot on a bed of embers. Other young men of the Men's House give proof of their skill walking on stilts or showing off their acrobatics. Musicians who play several instruments and masked dancers give the celebration the look of a carnival, where religious ritual, jokes, and foolishness all merge.

A DOUBLE DAY

Muluc is the ninth day of the holy Mayan calendar and it has two patrons: the god of water and jade, and the god of fire and sun. This double spirit is reflected in the ceremonies that accompany the celebrations of the Muluc New Year in which water and fire are brought together.

The Celestial Snake

Observe carefully the figure in the front on the left, his body splashed with red. He is wearing on his head a mask that has a three-pointed tongue and he is sprinkling purifying water with a rattlesnake. He is a high priest who is impersonating the heavenly sky which the Mayans perceive as an enormous two-headed snake. It is said that the snake is holding up the sky with his star-studded coils, sending out sun and rain from his fangs. That is why the Mayans consider the rattlesnake a sacred animal and refer to it with the same word that they use for sky.

The End of Katun

This is the most important and dramatic event of the Mayan calendar. It marks the end of a twenty-year cycle, or period which is what the word katun means. It is as if the end of a cycle were opening a deep pit in the orderly passage of time. The sun that sets on the eve of the end of Katun possibly may not reappear at dawn. Then darkness would engulf the Earth forever, and it would be the end of everything.

To prevent this from happening, it is necessary to carry out solemn ceremonies and to offer sacrifices to the gods. New twin pyramids have been erected in a suitable place that has been declared sacred. For eighty days, priests and novices alternate fasts with severe penitence. At sunset all the fires in the city are put out, dishes and household utensils are broken, while women, men, and children cover their heads with ashes.

In the fading light of dusk you hear in the distance a slow drum roll which is suddenly interrupted. You know that at that exact moment on the altar at the top of the Temple of the Great Jaguar, the executioner-priest, the *nacon,* has sacrificed a victim the people believed would fly to heaven to implore the pity of the gods. It is then that the planet Venus appears twinkling in the heavens. Suddenly a wild, triumphant racket of bells, trumpets, flutes, and drums explodes. It is the sign that on the next day a new dawn will rise and for another twenty years, a katun, the world is safe.

If the Earth Trembles

In Tikal it is quite normal to notice earthquake shocks from time to time. Most are of a very mild nature. It is said that they are due to the fact that one of the four *bacab* that hold up the heavens becomes tired and changes position. If this occurs at the end of katun it is not a good sign.

The "New Fire"

The celebrations in honor of the end of katun end with the ceremony of the "new fire." In the semi-darkness that covers the ceremonial center of Tikal, you suddenly notice the gleam of a faint flame stoked by an officiating priest. Little by little, fed by dry twigs and by the resin of copale, a brilliant bonfire flares up on which the young student-priests light pine torches which they pass from hand to hand throughout the whole city. The light of hundreds of stars appears to rise from the renewed firesides of the Earth to welcome with joy the rising of the moon in the sky.

31

The Flyers

Just to be able to attend the spectacular "dance" of the flyers (*voladores*) is worth a trip to Tikal. Dance? Yes, "dance!" Because the leaps into space with which the four acrobats, with ankles bound to long cords, descend little by little, from a high pole toward the ground is an authentic dance, moreover a sacred one. The symbols of a ritual are all there, right in front of your eyes. You only have to know how to read and understand them. The pole, painted in a greenish blue, 65 feet tall and thrust deeply into the ground, is nothing other than the silk-cotton tree (*la ceiba*). It represents the axis of the universe that joins the upper world to the lower one. The framework in the form of a pyramid is attached to the pole. A priest sits on top beating a drum to indicate the passage of the stars and time.

The four flyers, who are student-priests dressed in eagle feathers and crests, represent the four cardinal points, each with its own color. Blood red represents the east, the rising sun, the origin of life. Black is the symbol of the west, the night, the domain of death. White stands for the north, purity, the road to knowledge. Yellow is the color of the south, ripe corn, nourishment, the world of abundance. Down below the crowd cheers on the flyers as they control the slow unfurling of the cords to which they are attached. The color that touches the ground first represents a fortunate or unfortunate prophecy for the coming days.

ONE WORLD, IN FACT THREE

The Mayans have a genuine passion for magical connections. For them the visible world is only one part of the true world. Besides the Earth, which they believe is the back of a turtle or a giant alligator, two other worlds exist: the "upper" one, consisting of thirteen skies held by the same number of gods, and the "lower" one, divided into nine kingdoms ruled by nine gods. The Mayans see the world, therefore, as both one and three, and one and three are good, favorable numbers. Thirteen is also a good number and represents the hours of the day. Nine, which corresponds to the number of hours of the night, is the number of magic and of medicine.

The *Ceiba* and the *Moan*

In the forest you may see a tree that is taller than all the others. It is without question a ceiba. Don't touch it, it is sacred. Its roots sink down into the dark caverns of the hereafter, its leaves seem to fill the sky. In it lives the moan, a bird that is half owl and half eagle, which possesses the gift of seeing the future and the end of humankind.

33

The River Port of Yaxchilán

Yaxchilán stands in the midst of Mayan territory, but when you are there the feeling is one of being in some unknown region. This is not because of the look of the city, which more or less looks the same as other Mayan centers. The acropolises of Yaxchilán are built on a rocky ridge facing the left bank of the Usumacinta River. They may appear to you in the distance like the wings of a spectacular stage that overlook the landscape from a great height with its majestic terraced stairways.

But that is not what makes Yaxchilán unique. Its people's language, customs and traditions are very similar to those of the people of Tikal. What makes Yaxchilán different from the other Mayan cities is its peo-

ple's willingness to meet and do business with outsiders. Located strategically for connecting the Mexican Valley with Central America, its river port is the point of landing and departure of all the merchant expeditions that cross the Mayab. That is why in this corner of the forest you can find Mayan merchants carried on a kind of couch and surrounded by protective escorts. They come here to trade with other commercial travelers. Some of these merchant groups come from great distances. They might be dressed in unusual outfits and speak strange unknown languages. What is used as money? Everything from ceramic pottery to animal skins, from copper to precious stones, from seashells…to slaves.

COCOA AND THE NORTH STAR

When you see a Mayan with his body covered with black stains, he is without doubt a merchant. The stains are the symbol of the god of cocoa, which, used as money, is also the symbol of commerce. Black represents the north, associated with the god of the North Star, the travelers' guide.

The *Mezacpal*

You have probably noticed that the Mayans are capable of transporting very bulky and heavy loads on their back! The secret of how they manage to do this is hidden in a simple band, the *mezacapal*, made of leather, fabric, or cord, with which they encircle their forehead. To this is attached a heavily loaded basket or wooden frame. Could this be one of the reasons that the Mayans elongate the heads of their children? You will notice that the heavy loads are mostly carried by women and slaves.

The Great Cenote of Chichén Itzá

The city of Chichén Itzá, according to the Mayan calendar, is relatively "young." In fact it is a little more than fifteen katun old, although there are some who claim that it has existed forever. In truth in its territory there have "forever" been many large, deep wells, the *cenote,* which form lakes considered to be sacred and about which numerous legends have grown. Mayan warriors from far away have been gradually taking over the area. They claim that the seven demigods who gave birth to their clan had once lived here. Therefore, the city should properly belong to them. Whatever the case may be, the site is surrounded by a magic aura, and around the cenote these other Mexican Mayas carry out ceremonies that often climax in human sacrifices, especially of young women and of babies. Famous throughout the Mayab is the Great Cenote, site of many sacrifices. Frequent pilgrimages takes you to the site. You can join one to visit it. To go alone would be risky.

On moonless nights when the great rains have raised the water level, just in front of the Great Cenote priests practice their initiation rites for the new *ahmen.* The ahmen must first give proof of his visionary skills. Then he must submit to a series of painful tests before he is officially accepted as a true shaman. The symbol of his new role is a large tattoo on his back applied at the climax of the ceremony.

Water of the Cenote

For the Mayans there are several types of water. There is rainwater which descends from the heavens, beneficial and pure and black water of the cenote, well of sacrifices and dark passage to the subterranean world. Only when the two waters mix can you approach the cenote safely.

The Uay

If you observe the face of a Mayan priest during a ceremony, you will notice how it seems to transform itself to take on the features of a cat. This is the guiding spirit of the shaman, perhaps a jaguar, who lives in him and who shows itself in certain circumstances. Every medicine man has his own animal double capable of leading him beyond space and time into the regions where demons and gods live and where he gets his magical strength. When his cat-spirit succeeds in taking possession of the shaman, be careful. It's better to be far away.

The Observatory of Palenque

The night has to be special, transparent and clear, with the moon and the stars lighting up the sky. The sounds of the forest surprise you at every step: the croaking of the frogs, the call of the birds, the rumbling of the jaguar... the sudden silences! Then preceded by astronomer-priests who serve as your guides, you can venture in bright moonlit clarity up the steep stairs of the tower of the Palenque palace and attend a ceremony that has been held for centuries.

At the top of the tower, the astronomers closely examine the sky, studying the stars and the movement of the planets. After having selected and pointed to a celestial body, the head astronomer examines it carefully trying to establish its exact position with the help of a kind of telescope made from a hollow tube in which jade lenses, smoothed to the point of being transparent, have been mounted. Little by little the observations become more exact, the astronomers whisper numbers and names to a group of scribes all around the tower. These men record the data on a piece of bark, comparing the new facts with those of the past. The purpose of this night is to follow the passage of Venus from evening star to morning star and to discover the favorable or unfortunate meaning of the event. It is a delicate and solemn moment on which the future of the world depends.

Splendid Palenque

Palenque is located in the extreme west of the Mayab in an excellent raised position, on a platform surrounded by hills that tower over the Gulf of Mexico. Its buildings with their sloping roofs are crowned by elegant parapets or extensions, which make it appear from a distance as though it were suspended above the forest. From the royal palace there rises a tower 50 feet high, the tallest in the Mayan territory, which is used as an astronomical observatory. All around are spread pyramid-shaped temples and sanctuaries whose delicate decorations appear to give off their own light. To see Palenque is a joy to the spirit.

THE RABBIT ON THE MOON

The Mayans observe the world with enchanted eyes. On a night with a full moon in which you can distinguish the lunar "mountains" and "seas," the Mayans see in the sky, the mother of the gods. She is smiling at them kindly, holding a rabbit in her arms which she cradles tenderly.

Copán, the City of Science

Copán, "the beautiful," "the sweet," "the knowing." Even though it may not seem far on a map, in reality you have to cross almost half of the Mayab in order to get there. The journey is tortuous, broken up by difficult, rugged areas; treacherous rivers that are not always navigable; and by dense forests. Having finally arrived at your goal, in the center of a fertile river basin 2000 feet high, you are bewitched. You might be charmed by the unusually mild climate of the place. Or it might be on account of its spicy smelling air, borne by the cool breezes that come down from the pine-covered mountains.

You will also be attracted by the energy of its people. Copán is one of the most famous Mayan cities not only because of the beauty of its landscape, but because it is a cultural capital. Evidence of this is the great respect enjoyed by Copán's school for scribes where young noblemen from all over the Mayab gather to perfect their studies. The school is

a kind of national academy, the seat of periodic meetings of the greatest Mayan scribes and astronomers. Here rises the famous Stairway of Hieroglyphics in the center of the city. Its 65 steps serve as an open-air book decorated with more than 2,500 *glyphs* or symbols that tell the history of the city.

Writing: a Divine Gift

The skill of writing earns much prestige and respect among the Mayans for being placed under the protection of two divinities: the Rabbit god, who is associated with magic, and the Monkey god, guardian divinity of the Mayan civilization.

The Scribes, an Exclusive Caste

If you wish to see Mayan scribes at work, Copán is the ideal place, although it turns out to be not so easy to do. First of all, because forming even a simple *glyph* requires artistic talent and years of practice, the skills of the scribe are closely guarded. They hold the monopoly on writing. The scribes are the only ones capable of interpreting and passing down the history and knowledge of Mayan civilization gathered over the centuries. It is no wonder that scribes prefer to keep the secrets of their craft.

The Steles of Quiriguá

Quiriguá is located in the southeast of the Mayab a little to the north of Copán on the Motagua River. The city is not very large, but it is prosperous and adorned with genuine artistic gems. Much of its wealth comes from the mines in the hills behind the town from which excellent volcanic glass is extracted and exported as far as Tikal. Wealth also comes from jade, another important resource of the area which is sold everywhere.

But the real jewels of Quiriguá are its steles. These stone monuments, shaped with great accuracy, are slender and elegant. They contain altars at their base, which recall the shapes of animal-gods who, as in a large part of the Mayab, portray kings given bodily form in the stone and venerated as gods. Marvel of marvels of Quiriguá is the so-called Great Stele, which with its 36 feet of height, dwarfs every other stele ever erected in Mayan lands. The ideal moment to admire it is at dawn, when at its base the priests burn incense while chanting their prayers. But there is more. At the top of the Great Stele there stands an enormous glyph that bears the date which marks the beginning of recorded time. For the Mayans: that year is 3113 B.C.

THE FOURTH SUN

Why are the Mayans so obsessed with the measurement of time? Perhaps an old and rather disturbing legend can explain it. The world in which we live, so say the Mayans, is not the only one that the gods have created. Before this one there were three other worlds or Suns, which gradually were created and destroyed because they were imperfect. One world was dominated by animals, one by mud beings, and one by wooden beings. Our world, the fourth one, dominated by humans created from corn is also imperfect, and is therefore destined to be destroyed. When? According to Mayan forecasters precisely on December 22, 2012.

Jade, a Heavenly Gift

If you think that jade is a stone, you are mistaken. For the Mayans flint, an ordinary hard, heavy quartz is a stone. So is obsidian, a dark natural glass formed by cooling lava. But to the Mayans jade is not a stone, especially not the blue-green variety, the color of water and of budding flowers. Such beauty cannot come from the ground; it is without question a gift from the heavens.

Uxmal, Puuc Style

To visit the city-state of Uxmal, you need to push on to the extreme northwest of the country. Here the city stands in an area of low, wooded hills. It is a pleasant and inviting area but it has no source of fresh water. In order to overcome this obstacle the inhabitants of the city have created a clever system of cisterns, or reservoirs, for the collection of rainwater. This system guarantees a good water supply even in periods of drought.

With the aid of the god of rain, Chac, who is particularly venerated here, the Mayans have gradually solved the problems of urban development and growing population. Because of the generous supplies of water available, the city is in a constant state of growth and construction. This constant construction has produced in time an original architectural style (Puuc style) whose super-abundant, refined geometric decorations give the buildings a pleasing sense of lightness and movement.

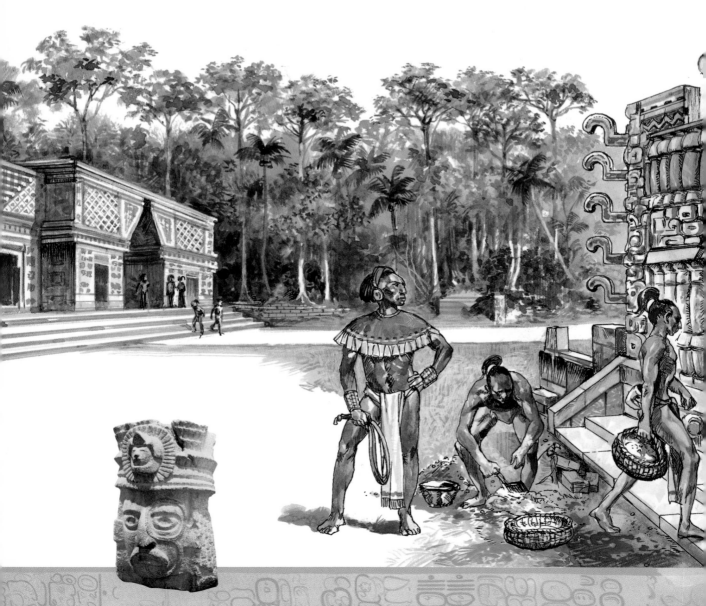

THE "TRUNK" OF CHAC

You certainly will note a frequent design in the Puuc style—an extension in the form of a hook, placed on the front and sides of a building. If you look carefully, you will note that these "hooks" are usually located in the center of a large-eyed, stylized face carved in the stone. It is the portrait of Chac, the heavenly god of rain, and the protuberance, similar to an elephant's trunk, represents his nose. Chac is venerated in all of the Mayab, but especially in the most arid zones where rain is awaited like a divine blessing.

The Arch of Venus

The Mayans call the planet Venus, "the great star" or "the wasp star." And they fear it because they believe it can announce war or misfortune. The arch that you catch sight of above the door on a left side of the palace is positioned to follow the passage of Venus and to spy on its movements.

War

The Mayans often start a war or at least a military action in order to capture prisoners to use as slaves or sacrificial victims. Or else, at times to conquer other peoples and territories. There is no question of war as just or unjust, good or bad action, but rather a useful one. Perhaps for this reason wars are so frequent in the Mayab. They break out unexpectedly and just as suddenly they stop. The war season coincides with the rains when the field work is abandoned and the farmers can get away from their lands. Usually the warring aristocracy promotes the war under the guidance of a military leader, the *nacom*, recruiting the citizens by force, and starts the action.

The ordinary warriors paint their bodies red and black, the colors of blood and death, while the leaders put on magnificent headdresses which indicate their rank as well as impress the enemy. The most commonly used weapons are the lance with a point made of obsidian or flint, and the *macana*, a sword with a wooden hilt and a blade also made of flint or obsidian. The shield, *pacal*, is made of wicker or wood, and covered with decorated cloth or leather.

The most injured and weak of the captured enemies are executed on the spot. The stronger ones are painted in white and black and taken as prisoners.

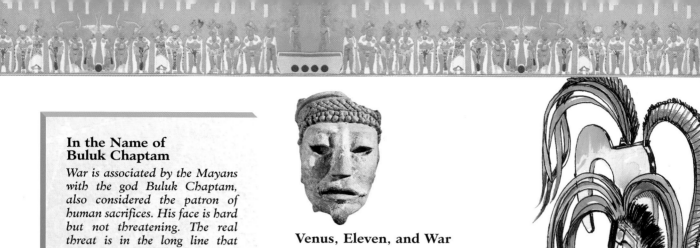

In the Name of Buluk Chaptam

War is associated by the Mayans with the god Buluk Chaptam, also considered the patron of human sacrifices. His face is hard but not threatening. The real threat is in the long line that descends from his eyebrows along his cheek—an unquestionable symbol of death. Buluk Chaptam is not, however, a simple god of war. He is the god of violent death, in battle or on the altar. He is represented with his right hand stretched out in a gesture of seizing his victim. Some images of the god show him in the act of starting a fire with a torch or striking with his lance. Better to keep one's distance.

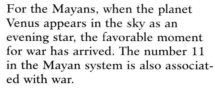

Venus, Eleven, and War

For the Mayans, when the planet Venus appears in the sky as an evening star, the favorable moment for war has arrived. The number 11 in the Mayan system is also associated with war.

Present-Day Tikal

If you don't mind roughing it a bit, it is possible to stay at a campsite near Tikal, which is now a national park. Standing among the ruins of Tikal's sacred sites, you feel the tremendous pull of both history and mystery. You are in the midst of the largest and perhaps the oldest of the Mayan structures.

Adding to the atmosphere of this strange and beautiful spot are the calls of the wild birds in the surrounding rain forest. Over 300 kinds of birds are protected here as part of a government conservation program. Take a guided tour to see parrots and toucans, monkeys and snakes, and maybe other rain forest wildlife as well.

Tourists Climbing One of the North Acropolis Pyramids

Climbing one of Tikal's pyramids will be one of the high points of your trip. Try to wear light cotton clothes and shoes with non-slip soles. A hat will help protect you from the sun, and be sure to carry a canteen of water. Getting up the long flights of steps sounds like hard work, but the marvelous view from the top of the pyramid will be more than worth the effort. Getting back down may be a little scary, but you can do it!

Northern Acropolis— Temple II in the Distance

On one side of the Great Plaza in Tikal's Northern Acropolis stands Temple II, seen here looming in the distance. This building is also known as the Temple of the Masks for the decorations on its stairway. On its wooden lintel is the figure of a standing woman in a long garment. If you visit New York's Museum of Natural History someday, you may see one of the original carved beams of this lintel. Many of the once-buried treasures of Tikal's temples are kept in the National Archaeological Museum in Guatemala City. A visit to this museum, which has rare Mayan artifacts, will repay you with close-up views of some fascinating artifacts.

Central Acropolis, Tikal

On the south side of Tikal's Great Plaza is a group of 42 buildings covering four acres. This complex is known as the Central Plaza. Built on several levels, most of the buildings are long and low. They contain hundreds of rooms, passageways, and courtyards. Believed to have been used as homes for the aristocracy, many of the buildings still lie buried under 50 feet of earth. However, what is visible of the cut-stone structures is impressive.

If you can manage it, try to visit the Central Acropolis on a night when the moon is full. Then Tikal becomes a mysterious silvery-blue city. You may be sleepy, but you will be glad you stayed awake to enjoy such a magical sight.

Giant Jaguar Pyramid

The Temple of the Jaguar Priest is located in Tikal's Central Acropolis. It is named after the figure of a fat man in a jaguar skin found inside the 180-foot structure. Here you will see above the entrance some of the best preserved decorations in the area.

Approach this temple with respect. In it was held the most sacred and private ceremonies in all of ancient Tikal. These ceremonies were attended only by the highest-ranked priests and the ruler himself.

Outdoor Market—
Chichicastenango, Guatemala

Chichicastenango, in the western highland has been the site of the Mayas' largest trading center since long before the Europeans arrived centuries ago. From Guatemala City take one of the many crowded buses that drive tourists to this exciting and colorful market on either a Thursday or a Sunday. That is when hundreds of Mayan descendants travel here from near and far bringing their products with them. Outstanding among their wares is the handwoven cloth with its brilliant colors and handsome designs. You will surely be tempted. As you wander around the noisy, bustling market, you can tell that it is more than just a trading center. It is a place for people to meet, exchange news and gossip and just enjoy themselves. You will too.

Village and Cultivated Field, Guatemala

The main crops of Guatemala are coffee, sugar, bananas, corn, and cotton. However, the country is also known for its spices. And as you explore the countryside, you are likely to see many small farms that grow a variety of spices. On this farm in the Petén, allspice is being dried in the hot sun.

So remember when you are enjoying your favorite spicy dish at home, one of the spices may have come from a farm you passed on your journey.

Stela at Quiriguá!

The ancient city of Quiriguá is in the eastern part of the Montagua valley. It is well worth a visit because of the number and size of its steles, now part of a 75-acre reservation. The steles are single slabs of carved and decorated red sandstone and range from 10 to 35 feet in height. You will be awed by the sheer massiveness of these amazing monuments and you may want to touch one of them. Don't. Each one is protected by heavy fencing.

Governor's Palace and Magician's Pyramid (Uxmal)

The Governor's Palace (left) and the House of the Magician (right) are located in the ancient city of Uxmal. As you look up at the Palace you will wonder at the skill of the ancient Mayans who carefully cut and fitted the 20,000 stones that make up the magnificent mosaic decoration of the cornice. Perhaps you will be lucky enough to be on the site on a sunny afternoon. Then you can watch the famous shifting patterns of light and shadow created by the unusual shape of the Magician's House. Your guide might tell you the story of the supernatural construction of this 93-foot-high pyramid in one day by a magical dwarf.

Some Important Dates

Preclassic or formative period – Covers approximately two millennia from 1800 B.C. to A.D. 250. The first Mayan agricultural communities settled along the coasts of the Pacific and the Caribbean. Between 900 and 500 B.C. the cultural influence of the Olmec civilization penetrated into the southern highlands of the Mayab, and it is to this people that such features as writing, the calendar, and the game of palla are owed. The first elements of Mayan civilization appeared with the rise of local centers where agriculture and commerce flourish, governed by groups of hereditary rulers and by the priest caste. At the end of this period the first signs of monumental architecture decorated in stucco begin to appear. The major Mayan centers of the period are Izapa and Kaminaljuyú.

Classical Period – This period lasted six centuries from A.D. 250 to 900. It marked the phase of the greatest development of the Mayan civilization. The rise in Mexico of the city-state of Teotihuacán set in motion a strong economic and political development in the Mayab. The Mayan cities in the center, like Tikal, used this concept of the city-state to establish strong territorial kingdoms with the aim of extending their sphere of influence toward the north Mayab and Central America. This led to a series of local wars for supremacy, which around the sixth century caused a temporary break in the development of the Mayan city-states.

The authority of Tikal over the central lowlands was challenged by the most famous city-states of the Mayan territory—Copán and Palenque, the capitals respectively of the southeast and the west; Yaxchilán and Quiriguá, which controlled the areas respectively of the Usumacinta and Motagua Rivers; and Uxmal and Chichén Itzá, the emerging cornerstones, respectively of the northwest and the north.

The entire Classical Period is characterized by a huge population and economic growth and by great cultural development.

The Crisis in the Ninth Century – Between A.D. 825 and 925, Tikal and a large portion of the Mayan cities underwent a rapid decline and were abandoned. Only the regions in the northwest and in the north, into which the Mexican Toltec people poured, appeared untouched by this process. There are numerous ideas concerning the causes of this sudden decline: epidemics, catastrophes, invasions, a series of wars, popular uprisings against the abuse of power on the part of the ruling classes, prophecies of doom and disaster. A reasonable theory is that the excessive population caused by the extraordinary economic development of the classical period put pressure on the limited economic resources of the territory and destroyed the environmental balance causing a series of disastrous famines. Lacking certain proof, the collapse of the Mayan civilization remains a mystery.

Post-classical Period – This era goes from A.D. 925 to the Spanish conquest. The Mayan cities in the north of the country that survived the ninth century crisis were ruled by the Mayan-Toltec dynasties. Around the eleventh century Chichén Itzá gave birth to a civilization which was dominated by the recurrence of human sacrifice.

In the thirteenth century, the control of the region passed into the hands of the city of Mayapán whose constant civil wars brought the region to the brink of ruin. When the Spaniards began the conquest in 1524, they met almost no resistance from the Mayan kingdoms.

Glossary

ahau Lord, honorific title that designates a king as well as high priests and which implies the idea of divinity

ahmen Priest endowed with prophetic powers, but also a healer and shaman

bacab Bearer, one of the four divinities that hold up the heavens

balche Beverage made from fermented corn and honey

ceiba Wild cotton tree, considered the central support of the universe, the cosmic tree

cenote Large and deep natural well of sweet water produced by the collapse of subterranean grottos

chicle Vegetal latex used either to produce chewing gum or the rubber used in making the balls for the game of palla

chili Spicy, red pepper

copale Vegetable resin used as incense

ex Masculine garment consisting of a piece of cloth passed between the legs and wrapped around the waist, a loincloth

glyph Image or sign representing a word, sound, or symbol, the basis of Mayan writing. The word hieroglyphic has to do with such a system.

haab Mayan civil calendar of 365 days

katun Period of 7,200 days corresponding to 20 Mayan solar years

kin Sun, day

macana Wooden sword with blade of either flint stone or obsidian

manta Feminine article of clothing, a top garment that consists of a large, generally embroidered tunic with openings for the head and arms

metate Concave stone used in the grinding of corn

mezacapal Band worn on the forehead making it possible for the Mayans to carry considerable weight on the back of their shoulders

milpa A field that can be cultivated after clearing and burning a portion of the forest

nacom Military chief

nacon Priest who does sacrifices

pacal Shield, usually made of wood or wicker, covered in leather

quetzal Rare Central American bird whose long, emerald-colored tail feathers are part of the symbols of power and holiness among the Mayan elite

sacbé (pl. sacbeob) Raised, paved street

tun 360-day cycle spread over 18 months, the basis of the Mayan solar year

tzolkin Holy year of 260 days

Voladores Priest-acrobats who, in the course of certain initiation ceremonies, hurl themselves into space, with their ankles tied to a rope, on a high pole symbolizing the cosmic tree

Further Reading

Baquedano, Elizabeth. *Aztec, Inca, and Maya.* (Eyewitness Books). Random House, 1993.

Black, Nancy J., and Turck, Mary. *Guatemala: Land of the Maya.* (Discovering Our Heritage series). Silver Burdett Press, 1998.

Chrisp, Peter. *The Maya.* (Look into the Past series). Raintree Steck-Vaughn, 1994.

Ellis, Katherine. *Maya.* (Degrassi Book series). Formac Distributors Limited, 1995.

Haynes, Tricia. *Guatemala.* (Major World Nations series). Chelsea House, 1999.

Lerner Publications, Department of Geography Staff. *Guatemala in Pictures.* (Visual Geography series). Lerner Publications.

Meyer, Carolyn, and Gallenkamp, Charles. *The History of the Ancient Maya.* Simon and Schuster Childrens, 1995.

Odijik, Pamela. *The Mayas.* (Ancient World series). Silver Burdett Press, 1990.

Putnam, James. *Pyramid.* (Eyewitness Books). Random House, 1994.

Index